Praise for 'From In

Very useful little guide to go ge

After many failed relationships, ... I mean many, my dear friend Kath bought me this book and said, "Paul you need to read this now!" Well after thinking "yeah of course I do", I gave in and have read through from cover to cover.

Wow what a fab little book!! Written in a very humorous but apt style, this book tells you exactly what you need to know to get the partner you have always wanted.
Paul Stacey, 22 Feb 2014

Great little guide to netting a lover!

This is a great little book, packed full of insightful messages and useful tips on how to start finding and attracting love. The chapters are short and snappy, each ending with Peter's `Stop - Action Points' which help to keep you on track. The advice is sound and relevant for anyone who wishes to feel better about themselves. Even if you haven't found romance by the end of the book, if you follow Peter's advice you will feel happier and more confident and it can only be a matter of time before your little black book starts filling up. '
T Yeatman, 23 Jan 2014

Inspirational read whether you're looking for love or not!
As a fan of the author's *'How To Do Everything and Be Happy,'* I thought I'd give this a read.

I was happily surprised by how much of it I found relevant and interesting. Peter Jones stresses that in order to become irresistible to others, it's important to like yourself first. He goes on to give achievable ways to do just this. And, because he draws on his own background and experiences, you feel like the author really knows what he is talking about. The book is easy to read, informal but informative and very funny in parts.

Worth reading for anyone who wants to feel a little less invisible, whether they're looking for love or not.
'Love To Read', 21 Feb 2014

Simply Irresistible

Hair appointment is booked, wardrobe has been de-cluttered and my new sofa is due any day! Have to say I only bought this book because I like Peter's writing style - I had no intentions of 'getting myself out there' - but this book makes you want to stop being invisible - blimey he's good!
    Shelley Wilson, 2 March 2014

So true, a wake-up call, and funny too

A great "*stop waiting for him/her to knock on the door*" book. Some great personal stories and checklists to shake you up. Watch this space! A recommended read.
    'Yorshire Lass', 19 March 2014

Read more 5-star reviews at amazon.co.uk,
and also at
FromInvisibleToIrresistible.com

From Invisible To Irresistible

Your Twelve Step Action Plan
To Attracting The Man Or Woman
Of Your Dreams!

By Peter Jones

soundhaven books
www.soundhaven.com

Published 2014, in Great Britain,
by soundhaven.com limited
http://www.soundhaven.com

Text Copyright © Peter Jones 2014

All rights reserved. No part of this publication may be reproduced, stored in a retrieval system, or transmitted in any form or by any means, electronic, mechanical, photocopy, recording or otherwise, without prior written permission of the copyright owner. Nor can it be circulated in any form of binding or cover other than that in which it is published and without similar condition including this condition being imposed on a subsequent purchaser.

Please visit www.frominvisibleioirresistible.com
for contact details

ISBN: 978-0956885630

British Cataloguing Publication data:
A catalogue record of this book is available from
the British Library

This book is also available as an ebook,
for your kindle, ipad, ipod touch, iphone, pc, mac...
Please visit
www. frominvisibleioirresistible.com
for more details.

*To Della, 'chance' meetings, and poetry seminars -
you're proof that this book might just work!
Much love
Peter*

To Valerie
Best wishes

x

Contents

TO BEGIN WITH… 1

CHANGING YOUR MIND 4

    THE NEW MINDSET FORMULA 5
    ACTION POINTS 10
    DESPERATION 13
    DEALING WITH OTHER DEMONS 21

CHANGING YOUR IMAGE 38

    OUT WITH THE OLD 40
    IN WITH THE NEW 45
    LOSING POUNDS 49
    SPENDING POUNDS 58
    RELEASING YOUR INNER THESPIAN 68

CHANGING YOUR ENVIRONMENT 74

    OTHER PEOPLE 75
    THE RIGHT SOFA 80
    GETTING OUT THERE 85
    START DATING AND STOP WAITING 91

YOU STILL HERE? 96

    FINAL REMARKS 97
    IF YOU'VE ENJOYED THIS BOOK… 99
    ACKNOWLEDGEMENTS 101
    ABOUT THE AUTHOR 102

ALSO IN THE SERIES 104

    CHANGE YOUR LIFE TODAY… 105

ALSO AVAILABLE 106

THE GOOD GUY'S GUIDE TO GETTING THE GIRL....................107

To Begin With...

Not that long ago, I walked into a crowded lecture theatre and sat myself next to the prettiest girl in the room.

If you've read any of my other books, or ever heard me speak, then you'll know this was how I met my wife, Kate – at a flirting course, some ten years ago. But this was a different lecture theatre. This was much more recent. And the subject being discussed wasn't flirting, it was poetry.

I ought to state for the record that I have absolutely no interest in poetry whatsoever. I have exactly one book of poetry in my house. It's currently helping to prop up my computer monitor. But as you've probably already guessed, I wasn't there for the poetry. I was there for the girl.

But what I didn't realise at the time – couldn't possibly realise – was that the girl I so casually sat myself next to, as though that were the only available chair in the room, had no interest in poetry either. She was there for me.

I've never been all that lucky in love. 'Luck' and I parted company long ago. Other people get lucky. I don't. 'Fingers crossed' has never really worked for me. Chance is not my friend. I prefer to leave nothing to it.

I realised long ago that if I wanted my life to be anything more than bearable, then it was necessary to figure out what I wanted, followed by a way to get that thing, all without relying on probability.

One of those things was 'love'.

So what of the girl in the poetry seminar? What became of her? That perhaps is a story for another time. For now I'd like you to concentrate on how we met.

You might think that we had very little say in the mutual attraction we felt. And whilst I would agree with you to a point, I, for one, had done everything I could to become a stunning specimen of poetry-hating manliness. My appearance, my wardrobe, my attitudes – even my apartment – they'd all undergone a series of self-imposed makeovers so that *this* special poetry-infused opportunity (and the moments that followed), could actually happen. Had I walked into that room two, maybe three, years earlier, I'm not so sure the lady in question would have given me a second look. Let's face it, she wouldn't have been there in the first place.

To Begin With... 3

Welcome to From Invisible To Irresistible.

If you've ever stood on the sidelines and watched people pair off, whilst wondering why no one seems to look at you twice, this book might be for you.

If your dating exploits only seem to get so far, or it feels like you're always the one doing all the chasing, this book is probably for you.

And if you're open minded, prepared to take a good hard look at yourself, make a few changes – if the end result means a more attractive you – then this book is most definitely for you.

Now then, could I interest you in some poetry?

Changing Your Mind

Brains, are amazing. Especially yours. Even mine has its moments.

I've written quite a lot about how amazing brains are; all three of my *How To* books[1] have chapters on how to use the 'power of focus' (what you choose to think about most of the time) to steer your life in a new direction. But it goes deeper than that. Believe it or not you can use the same or similar mental techniques to 'think' yourself more attractive *from the inside out*.

Let's take a quick look at some ideas that might be useful in your pursuit of love, and how a shift in mental gears can make you irresistible to the opposite sex.

---

[1] Visit peterjonesauthor.com/books for a complete list of all my titles

The New Mindset Formula

So there you are, sitting at home, when the phone rings. And just as you're about to answer you catch sight of the number on the caller display – and your heart sinks.

We've all had them from time to time. 'That' friend. You know the sort of person I mean. The friend who seems to have had more than their fair share of misfortune. When you met them they'd just been made redundant. They were embroiled in a long complicated dispute with their ex. Their kids, colleagues, landlord, neighbours, parents, police, pets, the postman, are all conspiring against them, on a daily basis.

And if you can summon the courage to answer the phone here's how the conversation might go:

"Hey! How are you?"

"Not too bad, I suppose. Yesterday was a difficult one."

"Oh, er, was it?"

"Well, it was the fifth anniversary of Bubbles."

"Bubbles?"

"My goldfish. You remember?"

"The one you had in college?"

"Yes. I was thinking about... how he died. So – tragic."

"Was it? I thought he was ten years old?"

"So young."

"Er, I suppose so."

"Nobody remembered. No messages. No cards. I sat here all of yesterday, just staring at the phone, waiting for it to ring."

You could feel sorry for them if... well, if there wasn't that nasty, spiteful part of you, that wonders just how much of this stuff they bring upon themselves. If you're anything like me, thoughts like that probably make you feel guilty.

Don't be. I've come to the conclusion that these people are toxic. They have the ability to take your otherwise pleasant mood, and sour it with their negativity. And it doesn't matter how strong you are, how determined you might be to stop them from dragging you down to their level, it's only a matter of time before they eventually win.

In fact the stronger you are, and the more you resist, the more you're buying into the game that's being played. They've discovered, consciously or otherwise, that this sort of 'poor me' attitude will get them the attention that they so crave. And when you finally realise that you can *never* do enough to put a smile on that persons face, and you quietly (or not-so-quietly) slip away, there'll usually be another sucker ready to take your place. And if there isn't, well there's always wallowing.

After all, wallowing has a lot going for it. It's reassuringly predictable and a darn site easier than trying to change things. What's more, during a good wallow it's usually possible to attribute the cause of your misery to someone else, thereby allowing you to stay miserable but blame free. Trust me. I know. This used to be me.

I'd walk around with a permanent cloud over my head, convinced that if I could just *find someone* – someone who'd love me – then finally, I'd be happy.

It took me a long time to realise that I had this completely the wrong way around.

If you were to take the younger, miserable me, flip open the top of my head and peer in, you could summarise my entire belief system into the following simple formula:

$$\text{ME} + \text{A GIRL} = \text{HAPPINESS}$$

As I didn't have a girl at the time, that was clearly the reason I was so unhappy. What I didn't realise until much later in life is that the formula – if there is one – should actually be the following:

$$\text{ME} + \text{HAPPINESS} = \text{A GIRL}$$

Become happy and you can have all the attention you'll *ever* want. You'll have found a way of attracting people to you, people who will want to stick around – forever, if they can. What's more this new structure of the formula works for almost anything that you currently believe you need to be truly happy. Become happy *first* and doors that were previously shut to you will magically open, opportunities will fall at your feet, 'lucky breaks' will spring up all around you.

Of course, being happy requires effort. Far more effort than being miserable. But it's several zillion times more effective and *no one* gets brought down in the process. No one.

And quite aside from the fact 'happiness' feels a whole lot better than misery, study after study has proved it's also healthier for you. Which is ironic considering it's also pretty contagious.

If you want that 'attractor factor', stop being such a bloody misery guts, and be happy!

So, how does one go about becoming happy?

There are those who will tell you it's simply a state of mind, a choice you make. Still others who will tell you that it's a by-product, fleeting, and that you should aim instead for 'inner peace'. And still others who'll tell you that to aim for happiness is foolhardy, that you should accept that life is made up of ups and downs. "Into every day," they'll say, "a little rain must fall."

I respectfully disagree. You can have happiness, and have it now (or very, very soon). Simply figure out what puts a smile on your face, and then do those things as often as you can.

Now I know how simple that sounds, so let me be the first to say that, in actual fact, mastering this deceptively simple concept takes some doing, and is the subject of many *many* books, seminars and workshops. And I should know. I've written one such book. And much of my time is spent delivering those talks and workshops[2], but in the meantime let's wrap this up into something you can use right now.

---

[2] To find out more pay a quick visit to howtodoeverythingandbehappy.com

Action Points

Throughout this book there are various Action Points. These boxes serve as Stop Signs. The idea is that you stop, address the action, and then continue.

Now clearly if you ignore the Action Point – the Stop Sign – it's unlikely that you'll be hit by a truck a moment later. Also I'm not going to pursue you through the remainder of the book, flag you down and issue you with a ticket and 3 points on your Amazon account. That's not going to happen.

Also, I've always been quite enthusiastic about 'ideas'. But whilst I like to collect and share ideas, I fully accept that you have just as much right to ignore them completely. I promise not to get annoyed with you for dismissing any suggestion (and these are only 'suggestions') I throw in your direction, if you promise to forgive me for being a little passionate, or teacher-ish.

That said, I'm assuming you bought this book because something in your head said, "Hey – I want to be more attractive…" and way back on page three, four, something like that, we agreed (well, you read it and I didn't hear you object) that you couldn't achieve this aim without putting in a little effort. So, as I'm writing the words, addressing the Action Points is your part of the deal.

With all that in mind here's the first Action Point of the book.

> **STOP! ACTION POINT!**
>
> Becoming Happy
>
> 1) Defence against toxic people: You can't help them. If you can, stay clear of them, or reduce their involvement in your life to a minimum.
> 2) Change your mindset
>
> **OLD MINDSET:**
> **YOU + SOMEONE ELSE = HAPPINESS**
> **NEW MINDSET:**
> **YOU + HAPPINESS = SOMEONE ELSE**
>
> 3) Become happy: Figure out what non-destructive things make you smile. Put a plan in place to fill your days with those things[3].

---

[3] And check out howtodoeverythingandbehappy.com for tips on how to do that.

Desperation

One of my happiness principles is 'figure out what you want, then figure out how to get that thing'. But simple though this principle might be to understand, it's not 'easy' to put into practice. Not by a long shot. The moment you try to change any part of your life you'll hit barriers, and sooner or later one of those barriers will be… you.

We all have them. Demons. Break away parts of our personality, formed at some point in our past, that have set up permanent residence inside our heads, with seemingly no other objective than to mess with our lives.

Nowhere does this seem to be more evident than when you're 'dating'. For instance, in the last chapter I told you how I'd got it into my head that I couldn't be happy unless I found myself a girlfriend. Tell me, does that sound a little desperate to you?

How 'desperate' are you?
So there you are, with your copy of *How To Start Dating and Stop Waiting,* steadily working your way through all the Action Points, painstakingly following all of my advice, safe in the knowledge that at some point, really *really* soon, everything's going to fall into place and –

hey presto! – you'll find someone, fall madly in love, and breathe a huge sigh of relief. But in the meantime you have this nagging feeling that it's all taking rather longer than you expected, certainly longer than you hoped. And, all around you, people seem to be getting hitched left, right and centre. People you didn't even realise *were* single are finding new partners in less time than it takes to send a carefully crafted two-word message. At this rate there's going to be no one left, you're going to be the only single person left on the planet, and you're beginning to feel ever so slightly, well, desperate!

I've been there. Oh, how I've been there. And let me tell you (in case you haven't figured it out already), desperation is *deadly*. Regardless of how breathtakingly attractive you usually are, desperation will cover you in a shroud and have potential suitors crossing the road to avoid you and running for the hills. It permeates your skin, your clothes, your very soul. It's like the worst body odour you can imagine – one that rubs off on everything INCLUDING your emails and text messages. And just like body odour you usually can't smell it on yourself – but boy howdy, can everyone else. Even if you think you've got a lid on it, chances are your friends and colleagues see you as a bug eyed, wild-haired freak, roaming the halls of the office building looking for anyone who might be 'available'.

Fortunately, there are some tell tale signs which even you won't be able to miss:

- Are you spending every available moment on dating websites trawling through pages and pages of profiles?
- Do you find yourself getting angry at the lack of responses you might be getting to your advances?
- Are you seriously beginning to wonder if everyone really is avoiding you?
- Do you find it difficult to look at people without wondering if they're single?
- Have you, in the last 48 hours, casually enquired, in the normal course of conversation, whether 'such and such' a person is single?

If you answered yes to three or more of these questions then I'm afraid you probably are coming across as 'desperate'.

The good news is we *can* do something about it.

For starters you might as well quit looking at those dating profiles, sending messages, or chatting up anyone you meet on your travels. Until you get this under control no one's coming anywhere near you.

Secondly, with the extra time you now have available, re-read the last section. Pay particular attention to the *mindset formula,* then put this book down (for a few days) and do something fun instead. Arrange a night out with some pals. Watch your favourite TV shows. Join an evening class or a club of some sort. Anything! Just do something that requires your full attention and is pretty much guaranteed to put a smile on your face – and (for the meantime at least) forget about *meeting someone.*

Next, write the following phrase on a label and stick it above your desk at home, the fridge door, or on your car dashboard:

I AM OK.

Whenever you look at the label remember that you are absolutely fine as you are. You *don't* need someone in your life. It would be nice, sure, but you're not somehow incomplete without them. You're complete now. Completely OK. Better than OK. You're lovely. And the more you believe that, the more others will believe it also.

If your facebook profile (or any other social media) shows your relationship status as single – remove it, or change the privacy options so only you can see it. It's better that other people wonder *if* you're single, than wonder *why* you're single.

Finally, in a week or so, when you're feeling more like your old self, come back to this book and consider resuming your dating exploits BUT in a far more laid-back, casual, almost dismissive manner. Here are some new rules to live by:

- Avoid talking about your dating exploits – even with friends. They don't need to know. It's no big deal. Dating is something you occasionally do for fun. But it's not the centre of your life.
- Avoid asking your colleagues if so-and-so in accounts is single (or any variation on this theme). Sure, feel free to wonder to yourself, for a passing moment, but let that moment pass. There's someone out there for everyone, but you don't need to wonder where they are.
- Accept that this is a long process. You're not going to meet anyone today. Tomorrow too is looking unlikely. But it'll happen someday. Quit worrying about the 'when', that's not your job.
- Your 'job' is to concentrate on being 'attractive' – in the truest sense of the word. That doesn't mean slapping on a tub of makeup in the morning or turning up to work in next to nothing. It does mean

being a nice, fun, happy person. Attractive on the inside. That's your new goal.

Desperation when dating

Annoyingly, even when you *start* dating someone desperation can rear its ugly head. Especially if the person you're seeing seems somewhat lukewarm.

There's this growing desire to 'bag 'em & tag 'em' – move things along as quickly as possible, get the 'dating' stage over with, and relax into the safety of a 'relationship'.

And therein is the solution to your problem. You need to 'relax' NOW, not at some point in the future. Because unless you do there's a strong chance you'll never ever make it to the relationship stage.

Tell tale signs of desperation in the early stages of the dating process come in the form of thoughts. Catch yourself thinking any of the following and you may have a problem:

➢ What can I do to *keep* this person?
➢ Should I call/text/email this person *yet/again*?
➢ What can I do to *make* this person like me?

It's those words *keep, make, yet,* and *again* – all signs that you're trying to push, pull or manipulate the situation in some way. It won't work. This is the voice of experience speaking, *both* as someone who's done a fair amount of desperate pushing and pulling, and as the party being pushed and pulled. Instead:

- Quit interfering! Relax! Let things progress naturally. By interfering you're actually making the outcome you desire less likely.
- Accept the fact that this might not lead to a full blown relationship – which I realise is very, very difficult to do, particularly if you've been single for a while, but if you can pull this off you'll remove any pressure and actually give things a fairly good chance of growing into something else. It's counter intuitive but one of the best lessons you'll ever learn.
- Enjoy your dates and time together. Lighten up. Laugh. Joke. Do something fun. Keep all your neurotic thoughts to yourself. Better still, leave them on the bus.

STOP! ACTION POINT!

Dealing With Desperation

Ask yourself the questions earlier in the section to determine whether you're coming across as desperate. If you are, utilise one of the cures below:

Before you find a date:
1) quit searching!
2) read the section entitled 'Mindset Formula' again!
3) concentrate on being happy.

When you find a date:
- quit interfering - relax!
- accept that this might not develop into a full blown relationship.
- enjoy dating!
- keep your options open.

Dealing With Other Demons

Desperation isn't the only demon hell-bent on scuppering your chances of a 'happy ever after'. Self doubt, self loathing, bitterness, jealousy – these are other demons that rock up periodically, or over and over, to prevent you from taking positive action, whilst making you less attractive in the meantime.

Let's tackle them one demon at a time.

Fear
What are you afraid of? That you might get hurt? Let me solve that for you now. You are going to get hurt. But… you will survive. So long as you take the usual sensible precautions with the people that you meet, the worst thing that is likely to happen is you might get your heart broken. Which sounds awful, I know, and hurts like hell, but you know what? Hearts mend. If you let them.

Fear is an interesting emotion. It's a defence mechanism designed to prevent you from doing anything that your subconscious has decided is 'dangerous'. Just how dangerous a thing appears is based upon your previous experience, what you can imagine, and whether or not it represents a fundamental 'change' to who or what you are.

As humans we're pretty much programmed to resist change. Part of the function of the large walnut-like sponge in your head is to maintain the status quo and keep you exactly where you are. It's a defence mechanism. A kind of inbuilt "If it ain't broke, why fix it?" process.

My personal resistance to change is incredible. Just wearing something a little different will set off that inner voice, it'll be screaming at me, telling me I'm totally bonkers, that no good can ever come of this radical change of image. I've learnt to recognise this voice. I use it to determine whether or not an idea or a course of action might actually achieve something. If I feel that resistance I know that an idea is likely to lead to change in my life, and I pursue it. But if I feel nothing – if the voice in my head is silent – then whatever I'm considering will probably have no effect at all, and might possibly be a colossal waste of time.

Perverse though it might seem, being aware of (and subsequently ignoring) the voice, my inner resistance, has become part of my mental tool box for making better decisions.

So perhaps the true reason for your fear, whether you've realised it or not, is because you *might actually get what you want*, and your psyche doesn't want that to happen.

Feeling the resistance? Excellent.

> **STOP! ACTION POINT!**
>
> Dealing with the Fear Demon
>
> What are you *actually* afraid of?
>   Consider the following:
>
> - Hearts mend.
> - We're programmed to resist change, and in this case the 'programming' might not be useful.

Negative self talk

There's a surprising amount of research on the subject of 'self-talk' and it turns out that negative internal chatter is far more damaging than you might think.

Your subconscious is highly suggestible. It has to be. That's how it works. And if it's told something frequently enough, it will eventually believe it. Which in turn will have a knock-on effect on your behaviour and the choices you make. This includes all the times <u>you</u> tell <u>yourself</u> that *you're stupid, you're tired, you don't feel well*, or *you don't like something.*

Don't believe me?

I have a friend who has a blog no one can remember the name of. Curiously it includes the word 'forget' in the web address.

Recently I worked with an actor who throughout rehearsals failed to exit when he was supposed to, because his cue line (which was intended to be ironic) was "I'm staying right here."

Then there's my fellow author, Della Galton, who took weeks to finish a particular short story a while back entitled, "You Never Finish Anything."

They're all examples of times where words that people say, or read, get lodged in the subconscious, and influence their behaviour. Powerful stuff.

This being the case, negative self-talk is a *really* bad habit to get into. And, given that there's often a queue of people lining up to point out our faults, why be one of them?

Instead, I encourage you to become your own fan club and use self-talk to your advantage. Next time you catch yourself saying something negative to yourself, immediately turn it around. So, for example, if you look in the mirror and find yourself thinking *my God I'm ugly – no wonder people run a mile*, counter it immediately with - *No! I'm an attractive man/woman – people want to be with me.*

Interestingly, the things that you tell yourself don't actually have to be true for your mind to take them onboard – and once your mind has adopted them your subconscious finds ways to make them a reality. This is the essence of the self-fulfilling prophecy.

> **STOP! ACTION POINT!**
>
> Dealing with the Negativity Demon
>
> Negative Self Talk is incredible damaging. Make a deal with yourself now. Next time you catch yourself running yourself down, counter it with the exact opposite phrase.
>
> For instance: *I'm an attractive man/woman – people want to be with me.*

Bitterness
Bitterness is desperation that's been allowed to fester.

The desperate individual begins to see a distorted view of an unfair world, where everyone and everything has conspired to ensure that they remain single and unloved.

Then anger sets in.

Self-help guru, Tony Robbins, teaches that anger is a reaction to someone or something breaking one of your 'rules'.

For example, if someone throws a rock through your window anger would be a natural reaction. Most people consider rock throwing in the vicinity of other people's windows unacceptable behaviour. So too is 'queue jumping', driving like an idiot, smoking in a non-smoking area, playing music really loudly in the middle of the night... these things will usually anger someone nearby because many people have 'rules' about these types of activities.

But many of us have 'rules' that few people, maybe nobody else, shares. Rules about what footwear is and isn't acceptable in certain establishments. What should or shouldn't be printed on the front of a t-shirt. How the tooth paste tube should be squeezed. Who should check pockets for tissues before they're put in the washing machine, and how long items should sit in the washing machine after the cycle has finished.

It's that word *should*. As soon as it creeps into your head you've created a rule, and you've opened yourself to the possibility of feeling angry if that rule is broken.

Should you still be single? After all this time? *Shouldn't* you have found someone by now? *Should* the world of dating work like it does? *Shouldn't* it be a darn sight easier? *Shouldn't* that person over there be attracted to something other than muscles, money, or mammaries? Shouldn't they realise that you're right here, right now? That you're exactly what they *should* be looking for? *Shouldn't* they?

Hard though it may be to hear, the answers to these questions are irrelevant, because they change nothing. Neither you nor I get to make the rules. Regardless of whether we *should* be allowed to make them.

To paraphrase Sir Terry Pratchet, "there is no justice, there's just you." By which I mean you're wasting time if you choose to spend any of it thinking about how the world should be. Instead, accept the world for what it is; there's you, me, and how things actually are. That's what we've got to work with. Nothing else.

Resentment

A close cousin to bitterness is resentment. Where bitterness is a sort of general, internal feeling about the injustice of it all, resentment is usually directed at someone or something. We have thoughts that start along the lines "I wouldn't be in this situation *if...*"

I used to be pretty good at feeling resentful towards my younger self. If he'd just got out of bed a little earlier, had a little more confidence, asked that girl out, moved out when he had the chance, been a little more responsible, thought things through for a little longer...

Like a broken record player[4] I'd replay these thoughts over and over in my head, round and around, driving myself ever-more crazy. Needless to say, no good could come of it. It happened. And until someone invents time travel, it won't un-happen, no matter how many times I replay those events.

But I can stop it from *continuing to happen.*

A more spiritual man might tell you to practice forgiveness, along with the acceptance we spoke of earlier. I'm going to offer you an alternative. If the resentment you're feeling is a direct result of someone, or something, or an incident that happened in your past,

---

[4] Kind of like a CD player, but bigger, and way cooler than all your new fangled techy gismos – you young whipper snapper!

then aren't you, in some way, letting that incident or that person continue to exert their power over you?

Many parents soon figure out the way to deal with a screaming toddler is to simply deny that child the very thing they want the most; attention. The same can be done with the past or whatever's causing you resentment. Pay it no more attention. Concentrate on something else. On what you want. Eventually, like the toddler, the resentment will stop.

Given all that, what are you going to do now?

> **STOP! ACTION POINT!**
>
> Dealing with Bitterness & Resentment
>
> Bitterness:
> - Bitterness is desperation that's been allowed to fester and become angry.
> - Anger is a reaction to someone breaking our 'rules'.
> - We don't get to make the rules! Accept the world for how it is. Figure out how the world *actually* works (rather than how it 'should') and devise a better strategy.
>
> Resentment:
> - Similar to bitterness.
> - Usually directed at someone or something, maybe even ourselves, and often something that happened in the past.
> - You can stop resentment in its tracks by denying that person or incident any more attention.

Jealousy
Jealousy is a strange emotion. It can seem completely rational, and totally irrational all at the same time. It can take you by surprise or be constantly lurking in the background. Some people will try and tell you that a certain amount of jealousy is a good thing, but I've always found it to be one of the most destructive relationship demons there is, constantly whispering its lies whilst blinding you from anything that might convince you of the contrary.

For the longest time I never understood jealousy until a friend pointed out that it's usually one of the demons we've already discussed, albeit in another guise. Most of the time it's *fear* – fear of losing the attentions and affections that we've been enjoying up until now – other times it's *anger,* a resentment directed at someone who has the life we want.

Let's deal with that anger first.

A few pages back we learnt that anger was the result of someone breaking a rule. In this particular case the rule that's been broken might be 'having a life which we deserve more' – but sadly, like many of the rules we come up with, we haven't actually been given the authority to make or enforce it. That's not our job. And wishing it won't change anything.

In fact, the very act of wishing things were otherwise – over and over and over again – is a tell tale sign that this is resentment. And, as we know, the way to deal with resentment is to take away the power it has over us by taking away the attention it craves.

But what if our jealousy is fear?

Earlier in the book we discovered that fear can be a defence mechanism, a warning that our subconscious considers something dangerous.

In this case it's warning us against potential loss. "Continue down this path," our subconscious is saying, "and all that affection and attention you've been enjoying will suddenly end."

Just knowing our jealousy is fear can sometimes be enough to dispel a jealousy demon entirely. Ask yourself: Is this fear justified? What exactly is the other person doing that makes you feel fearful? How likely is it, really, that you might lose the affections you've been enjoying until now? If your answers to these questions are "not really", "nothing" and "extremely unlikely" that jealously demon is probably already packing its bags.

But what if those fears *are* justified? What if there's a very real chance that the apple of your eye might be stolen away by another? Or what if, no matter how illogical and unlikely it is that you'll lose this attention you crave so much, you just can't shrug off the green eyed monster?

Three more steps come to mind:

Firstly, talk about it. In a constructive way. Rather than "I don't want you talking to that skanky harlot any more!", try going for something a little more honest; "I'm really worried that I'm going to lose you."

Second, man-up, and take responsibility for your part in this current drama. In particular, remind yourself that all these demons we've talked about make you significantly *less attractive*. The irony of jealousy is that the very act of being jealous is often enough to drive someone away and bring about what you're ultimately afraid of. And I speak here as someone who's been both the perpetrator and victim of this type of jealousy.

Finally, take that label you created in the last section and rip it up. It obviously wasn't big enough. Instead find a piece of paper approximately eight foot by four, and after you've added the three words below, paper it to a wall where you will see it several times a day:

YOU ARE OK

You are a grown adult. You are independent. You don't need to rely on someone else for your survival. Your emotional wellbeing is not dependent on having someone else in your life. If you're in some kind of relationship then that lucky person is your 'plus one' – they are in no way your 'other half'. Certainly not your 'better half'.

Go right back to the start of this chapter and re-read the section on the New Mindset Formula. Be happy with yourself first, THEN find someone to share your life with.

Phew! Let's wrap this up into some cosy bullet points.

STOP! ACTION POINT!

Dealing with Jealousy

Jealousy is another demon in disguise:

Anger:
- Reaction to a rule that has been broken.
- You don't get to make the rules.

Resentment:
- That someone else has the life we want.
- Deny that resentment the attention it craves.

Fear:
- Ask yourself if your fears are justified.
- Discuss your fears in a positive way.
- Examine your role in the current dilemma.
- Remember: Demons are unattractive – you might bring about the very thing you fear most.
- Remember: You are OK! You don't *need* anyone else to survive. Re-read the New Mindset Formula (at the start of the book).

Changing Your Image

So if the last chapter was about changing from the inside out, this chapter's all about changing *from the outside in.*

There are few things in this world able to boost your confidence quite so much as looking in the mirror and seeing someone you like the look of – just as looking in the mirror and feeling disappointed with your reflection has the ability to stamp out any shreds of confidence you might have been able to gather together.

Appearances matter.

And even if they don't matter to you, they matter to other people. You sometimes hear it said that people are shallow, that we should take time to 'see past the surface', that we 'shouldn't judge a book by the cover' – as someone in the book selling business I can tell you now that people judge books, and everything else, by the cover.

And is that so wrong? We're visual animals – hard wired to find healthy, child-rearing mates attractive. In a split second your subconscious is able to make decisions and assumptions based on a colossal amount of information coming in through five possible senses and cross referenced with all your previous experiences – it's a remarkable process, one that we can use to our advantage.

Now I'm no fashion expert by any means but fortunately for you, I don't have to be, changing your image is far simpler than you probably realise.

Out With The Old

Many years ago, when I was a naive young man in my late teens, early twenties, I had long hair. And when I say 'long' I'm not talking about an unruly mop that occasionally fell into my eyes, I'm talking about a mass of long flowing wavy locks that had an intimate relationship with my shoulders, and could easily reach the centre of my back when I stepped out of the shower.

I'd like to tell you that my mane was fairly typical amongst my peers, especially given that it was the eighties and every footballer or rock star worth their salt was sporting a similarly styled barnet. I'd like to, but I can't. Because it wasn't the eighties. It was the nineties.

Still, that didn't stop me, and despite frequent requests to get my hair cut (mainly from those people who considered themselves in some sort of position of authority) I persisted with 'the hair' because I was reasonably certain that it looked 'cool'.

How did I know? Because people had told me. Well, one person had told me. Maybe two. But they were *women*, and at the time that's all that mattered, and I clung to those compliments for dear life hoping that their opinions were the norm, rather than the exception.

Then one day I saw myself.

Shortly after my thirtieth birthday I was invited to a friend's wedding and unbeknown to me someone captured the whole event with a camcorder. A few days later I was treated to a viewing and for the first time I saw myself as everyone else did. And Oh My God.

The gaunt, pale faced man with the goatee beard and ponytail was not the young artisan I thought I was. Those 'thick flowing dark curly locks' were nothing of the sort. Instead they were a receding, thinning, greying, straggly mess, scragged back into a ponytail. And that's if I'm being kind to myself and limiting myself to just four adjectives. Those two ladies – or maybe just one – who'd told me that my hair was 'cool' were either lying, or more likely, it had only been true ten years earlier, and possibly only for them.

It's difficult to communicate the level of embarrassment and humiliation I felt. A part of me wanted to take that video, and every other copy that had ever been made, and erase the footage. But it wasn't the video that was the problem. It was me. Me and my stupid hair.

What happened next? The short answer is I got a hair cut. If we ever meet I'll tell you the slightly longer version, but for now let's cut (if you'll forgive the pun) to the chase; I lost the hair and an interesting thing happened.

People noticed me.

They didn't just notice me either. After the initial double take and inevitable comment about 'how much younger I looked' and how 'they never really liked the long hair', they took a second look, both at me and everything I was involved with. It was as if, having been forced to update their mental image, they took the opportunity to reassess everything they knew, or thought they knew, about Peter Jones. And for the first time, in a long time, the feedback was positive. How do I know? Did one, perhaps two, ladies tell me so? Oh no. Nothing so mundane.

Overnight my life changed for the better. People took me more seriously. I won clients with little or no effort. I doubled my fee and still got more work than I could handle. Even the fairer sex started to pay me more attention. And all I'd done is gone and got a hair cut. Looking back, I wish I'd done it five or even ten years earlier.

Is it time you had a rethink?

You know what's coming next I'm sure: If you have a particular hair style, a pair of glasses, a brand of makeup, a deep tan (fake or otherwise), or anything else that you've persisted with for *years*, just stop for a moment, and in the privacy of your own head ask yourself *why*?

Go ahead. Do that now, then find the answer below that closest matches your own.

"It took me forever to figure out what works – this is it!"
Really? Perhaps it's time to accept that it *did* work, at some point, but that it might not be working now. Fashions change. People change. We need to change with them.

"It's what makes me different!"
That's true. How's that working out for you?

"I like it!"
Well good for you. But does anyone else? Have you asked them for an honest opinion?

"Two people said they like it too!"
Two!??! Two people!?? What, recently?

"I don't care what people think. I'm keeping it."
And that's just fine. Especially if you want to remain exactly as you are. That is your end game isn't it?

Let's take some action.

STOP! ACTION POINT!

Get shot of old image-habits
that might be holding you back.

1) Ask yourself if there's any part of your image that's particularly unusual, or that you've maintained for a long time.
2) If the answer's yes, pour yourself a stiff drink, then find someone – maybe two independent 'someones' – who will give you an honest answer.
3) If the general consensus is anything less than favourable (a half-hearted "it's OK" coupled with a shrug does not count as a favourable response) seek out the assistance of a professional, and change it.
4) Prepare to be amazed.

In With The New

I've got a fridge magnet that declares to the world that 'you can't control everything. God put the hair on your head to remind you of that.' Respectfully, I'd like to disagree.

Things move on. Not necessarily that quickly, but they always do. And 'facts' that you have held on to for years might no longer be true.

For instance, when I was growing up it was generally accepted that there were nine planets in the solar system. Now there are only eight, and *five* – possibly more – *dwarf* planets.

Back on earth (and slightly more relevant to the issue at hand) it's generally accepted that we might develop the odd wrinkle, that we might have to hold the newspaper at arm's length to read it, and that men, most of us anyway, will start to experience hair loss, and that there's very little we can do about it. Not without embarking on some pretty frightening surgery. Or worse still, some sort of wig.

But like those planetary facts I spoke of, these things might not be true either.

And how do I know this? How do you think?

Though I rarely bring the subject up at dinner parties, I'm not ashamed to admit that a couple of years back, dismayed at my rapidly thinning hair, I went in search of a cheap, safe, non-invasive, natural looking solution and I was delighted to discover that I didn't have to go far.

Here in the UK, in recent years, selected pharmacies have begun trials of 'hair retention' tablets. One daily pill can put a halt to any further hair loss, and in some cases – me being one of them – causes new hair to grow back.

I'll admit it's a slow process. The tablets didn't work overnight. Rather, it's like turning round having walked several miles in the wrong direction, and starting the long trek back. But two years on and my hair is noticeably thicker.

There are those who raise an eyebrow when they discover I'm popping tablets to re-grow my hair. That eyebrow communicates many things. Perhaps they think I'm vain. Perhaps they think it's unnatural. Perhaps they think I should be embarrassed. I can understand those thoughts. I wrestled with them myself until I remembered the many, many bottles and jars of makeup and creams and dyes and lotions that my wife used to stack on four shelves in the bathroom. I don't remember her being embarrassed. I do remember her being beautiful. And if when she looked into that mirror she saw the person that I used to gaze upon, then I'm sure that must have given her a lift in the morning, put a smile on her face, and made it easier for her to tackle the day.

The point here is not the use of cosmetics. It's not even about hair, or hair loss. It's that time marches on, and that things that our parents considered 'facts' might no longer be the case.

Whether you're losing your hair, growing it in strange places, lost without your glasses, plagued by acne, skin discolouration, or daren't smile for fear of revealing crooked teeth, or no teeth at all, there are *solutions*. Many, many solutions – and in a few months there'll be many more.

Do yourself a favour; forget what you *think* you know and do some research.

> **STOP! ACTION POINT!**
>
> Update what you think you know.
>
> Thanks to the unstoppable force that is science and commerce, new products and processes come on to the market every day solving a variety of image-related issues that, until now, you might have thought you were stuck with.
>
> Do some careful research and see what's new[5]. You might be surprised.

---

[5] It goes without saying that you should be very cautious of buying 'miracle drugs' from the internet. In the case of my hair retention tablets, I wouldn't feel comfortable getting them anywhere other than my pharmacy where they ask me a battery of questions each and every time I go and monitor my progress.

Losing pounds

When I was a much younger man, the only pounds I ever had to worry about were the ones that should have been in my wallet. 'Fat' wasn't a word that was ever used in connection with me. I was the living embodiment of 'tall' and 'skinny'.

Even in my twenties, when I was mostly living on a diet of pizza and beer, where most people have a 'bottom' I had a 'place where my legs met'. Girls would tell me how lucky I was. Guys would question my ability to lift a bag of sugar. I'd just shrug, convinced that I'd never lose my ability to hide behind lamp posts or squeeze between railings.

How wrong I was.

I met my wife-to-be in my mid-thirties. The fact that I met Kate at all was something of a minor miracle, but her arrival in my life coincided with another miraculous event: I'd started to put on weight.

In a matter of months I somehow went from ten stone eight (148 pounds) to thirteen stone (182 pounds). People started to tell me how 'well' I looked. Occasionally I was described as 'cuddly'. And as Kate and I curled up in front of the TV to munch our way through a family sized bar of chocolate, she'd rub what she fondly referred to as the 'Buddha Belly'. It was almost enough to ruin my appetite.

Almost – but not quite.

As the months passed my weight crept ever upwards. My chins (plural) got ever bigger. Eventually I no longer felt comfortable being naked in front of my fiancée.

And that was the turning point.

Not the naked part – the fact that my girlfriend was now my fiancée. And on hearing the happy news one of my colleagues asked me when I was starting my diet.

"Diet!" I asked, with a mixture of indignation and confusion. What had diets got to do with marriage?

"Of course diet," she said. "You're never as slim as the day you get married!"

This was news to me, and something of a shock. And although the logical, adult part of my brain was quick to dismiss this as utter nonsense, another part – the part that has always been ready to believe anything negative or damaging – had already adopted this as a Universal Truth. I had only a few months to lose those pounds that I still thought of as 'extra' – or they would be mine *forever*. The clock was ticking.

It was nonsense, of course. But maybe you've been there. Bouncing from one diet to another in an effort to avoid what seems to be the inevitable – 'you will never be as slim as you once were'. Maybe you're at that point now, in which case you're probably familiar with a couple of other 'Universal Truths', namely that diets and exercise are miserable, soul destroying ways of losing weight, and if you stop either one for a millisecond then those grams that you worked so hard to shed come straight back the moment you so much as look at anything vaguely tasty.

There are few things in this life as cruel as how the human body manages its weight. At least that's how it feels. And I don't know about you, but there's only so much heartache I can take. After a couple of years of running in my lunch hour – returning to my desk hot, frustrated, and not the slightest bit lighter than the day before (or the week before, or any of the preceding months) – I finally threw my heart-rate monitor in the bin and went in search of a pain-free, exercise-free, scientific way to restore my trim figure.

And did I? Did I discover the secret to effortlessly maintaining my weight? Yes. Yes I did. And the secret – if there is one – is to make many, many small, painless changes to the way you approach eating, and watch the benefits add up.

Now sadly I haven't space in this book to go into each and every one of those changes, but that's OK because I don't actually need to. I've *already* written a book on the subject of weight management[6]. But in the meantime, let me give you just one tip that will utterly blow your mind. One that really worked for me, and restored me to the slender chap I am today.

The Oil Diet

Welcome to possibly the strangest 'diet' in the western world. I've tried a few odd things over the years on my quest for 'eat loads and stay slim' nirvana, but this is probably the weirdest.

The first thing to understand is that the 'Oil Diet' isn't really a diet at all. It doesn't ask you to count calories. It doesn't ask you to limit the amount you eat. It doesn't forbid certain foods or food groups. It merely asks you to be really strict with yourself for two hours each day.

And to drink two tablespoons of a near-flavourless oil.

So here's what to do:
1) *Decide in advance what time each day you're going to do the diet.* You need two hours when you can be completely strict with yourself. What you eat or drink the rest of the day is completely up to you, but

---

[6] *How To Eat Loads And Stay Slim,* co-authored with Della Galton, is available in audio, paperback and as an ebook. Find out more at howtoeatloadsandstayslim.com

Changing Your Image

for those two hours make sure you follow these eight steps precisely. Most proponents of the diet tend to do it either first thing in the morning or last thing at night – that way you're asleep for one of those hours.

2) *Use a clock* – The first and final hour of this regime are there to prevent the calories in the oil from being associated with anything you might have eaten, or might eat, before or after. If you're used to snacking or drinking pretty much constantly throughout the day, these two hours can really drag (another reason why I like to be asleep for one of them). For this reason don't estimate the time – use a clock! You might find setting a reminder on your phone useful.

3) *Begin the first hour* – Stop eating and drinking. <u>Absolutely</u> <u>nothing</u> (with the exception of unflavoured water) can pass your lips. This hour is a buffer so that the calories in the next stage don't get associated with anything you may have eaten earlier. For the same reason you mustn't smoke, brush your teeth, chew gum, or do anything else that might involve a flavour. If you break this rule you risk triggering a flavour-calorie association which will raise your set-point, ultimately causing you to <u>GAIN</u> weight.

4) *Drink two tablespoons of a near flavourless oil* – Measure out two tablespoons of near-flavourless oil into a glass (more on what oils in a moment). Top up your glass with three or four times as much water, and then swallow the whole lot down immediately (don't leave the liquids to separate). It's nowhere near as unpleasant as you'd think. It should feel exactly like drinking a glass of water.
5) *The second hour* – Continue to abstain from all food, drink and anything other than plain unflavoured water, for another hour. Again, this is a buffer. Again use a clock.
6) *Be really, really strict with yourself* – I really can't stress this enough. This is probably the only diet which will ultimately make you gain weight if you screw it up!
7) *Do something else!* – You don't have to sit there on your hands with tape over your mouth. You can still read, watch TV, go for a walk, call a friend, go to the gym, listen to music, sleep!!
8) Repeat daily until you reach your target weight.

Which oil you use is crucial to the success of the diet. Put away that extra virgin olive oil – that won't work. Neither will that fat free sunflower nonsense. The oil needs calories, but no flavour.

I use the 'mild & light' version of a popular brand of olive oil. It's mild and light in *flavour* – but the calories are the same as regular olive oil, which is very, very important. Apparently you can also try refined walnut oil, or refined coconut oil (the refining process reduces some of the flavour), light hemp oil, or safflower oil but I haven't done this myself as yet.

The oil diet actually has a number of side effects. Here's a list of them, and what to do if you notice them.

1) *Indigestion* – This hasn't happened to me but some people find that they suffer indigestion after drinking the oil. If this happens the advice is to cut down on the quantity for a day or two. This gives your body time to develop the enzymes it needs to digest the oil.
2) *Better skin* – Oddly, many people report better skin, less acne, silkier hair. If this happens be sure to toss your head to draw maximum attention to it, and to wear a smug expression at all times.
3) *Better sleep* – Some people report better sleep (possibly because of the high omega 3 content in some oils). That's almost reason enough to give this a go!
4) *Bloated feeling after eating* – A few days into the diet you might find that you feel bloated after eating

– like you're going to explode. This is actually the diet at work! Having lowered your set-point you'll feel fuller, faster. Meals that you once considered normal size are now too big. There are three solutions. Firstly, cut back the amount of oil you're using to one tablespoon for a day or two. Secondly, stop eating when you feel full. Finally serve less in the first place.

I'm not going to lie to you. I'm aware how completely bonkers this all sounds. When I first read about this 'diet' I was certain that it must be a ruse. But I've used it many, many times, and always with the same positive results.

If you're interested in the science behind how and why this diet works visit howtoeatloadsandstayslim.com and search for 'fatometer'. I also thoroughly recommend Doctor Seth Roberts' book (The Shangri-La Diet[7]) which covers all of the above and much, much more, as well as my own book *How To Eat Loads And Stay Slim*.

---

[7] ISBN-13: 978-0-9568856-1-6.

> **STOP! ACTION POINT!**
>
> Shed some pounds!
>
> - Be brave: Give the oil diet a try! (Stick rigidly to the rules)
> - Familiarise yourself with the science behind how hunger really works by visiting the *How To Eat Loads And Stay Slim* website and searching for *fatometer*
> - Try out some of mine (or Della's) other painless weight control tips mentioned on the same website

Spending pounds

Hard though this might be to believe, I used to be a bit of a disaster in the fashion department. If there's a fashion gene, I didn't get it. Other people stand in front of a mirror and know instantly whether the colour of the shirt they're wearing complements their complexion, whether that pattern is clashing horribly with their trousers. Other people know whether the cut of a garment is flattering or fattening, I... don't. To put it in terms you might be familiar with, I'm the person who's never quite sure whether my 'bum looks big in this', or whether my bum is just big.

I put this down to two reasons:

Firstly, I suffer from a general lack of 'fashion confidence'. I tend to be put off by anything that takes me outside my comfort zone. I used to pick clothes based on whether or not I received a 'negative reaction' from people I like. Consequently, I usually ended up choosing clothes nearly identical to those that I already own, which in the ever changing world of fashion is a bit ridiculous. Isn't it? You see – I have absolutely no idea what I'm talking about.

Secondly, if you haven't already guessed, I actually have virtually zero interest in men's fashions. To me the primary function of the items in my wardrobe has always been to keep me from feeling the cold. If they do so whilst giving me somewhere to keep my keys and loose change so much the better. The idea that they might also be used to attract someone of the opposite sex isn't lost on me, it's just that I'm not entirely certain what the opposite sex wants to see.

Which is why I called in a professional.

Janine was the first of several Image Consultants I've employed over the years. This was back when TV makeover shows were in their infancy, and more likely to focus on restyling your house than your wardrobe. I was completely upfront with my reasons for wanting to hire her services, and my honesty was probably one of the reasons why she quickly felt comfortable enough to dispense with diplomacy and declare my current image dull, boring, overly conservative and doing me no favours whatsoever. And whilst I reeled from the shock of this revelation (I knew the situation was bad, I just hadn't realised how bad) she rummaged through my drawers and chucked out every item of clothing I owned – with the exception of one shirt that she found at the bottom of the wardrobe, lost and forgotten, thrown there in frustration when it had become too short in the arms.

"Put this on a moment," Janine commanded, then stepped back whilst I did so. It looked ridiculous. Or so I thought.

She stepped forward, rolled up the sleeves, undid one more button than I would normally consider appropriate, stepped back and with one hand on her hips declared that I was already looking "much better." I think I probably blushed.

Which brings me rather nicely on to how I chose Janine in the first place.

Of the dozen or so Image Consultants I'd found, none of them really seemed to offer what I was looking for. Most offered their services to companies to assist in developing some sort of corporate dress code. A few were available privately to career-focused clients to help spruce up their professional wardrobe, but none of them offered a fashion makeover designed to put me in clothes that women might want to rip from my body in the throes of passion.

But then most, if not all, of the consultants on my list were self employed and female. And of those who'd had the foresight to put a photo on their website there were a few for who I'd have been very happy to take on the role of 'boyfriend', rather than 'client'. Which is why I picked Janine. Not because I wanted to employ her services under false pretences (it turned out she was married) but because I reasoned that any woman I liked the look of would put me in clothes that she herself would like to see me dressed in.

Did it work?

You tell me: Less than eighteen months later I was married, to a similarly career-minded woman, and whilst Kate never told me that my faded blue shirt, with the sleeves rolled up, and one too many buttons undone, had been her primary reason for marrying me, perhaps it had played its part in promoting me from 'nervous guy sitting next to her on a flirting course' to 'potential boyfriend material'.

One thing I am sure of – picking Janine on the basis of how I felt about her as a potential girlfriend, rather than her professional qualifications, definitely wasn't a mistake. And how do I know this? Because I've tested it. More than once.

Maybe a year or so after Kate's funeral, when I was ready to consider dating again, I looked in the mirror and no longer saw the young, laid-back, casual smiley guy who'd caught my wife's heart. Instead I saw a middle-aged man who seemed more than a little frumpy, grumpy, and in somewhat desperate need of some rumpy-pumpy.

But that was OK. I knew exactly what to do. I dug out Janine's number, and called it. It rang. And rang. And rang. No answering machine kicked in.

Not a problem. I bashed out a quick email and sent it. Only to have it returned seconds later.

So I scoured the internet. But her website was gone.

Fortunately though, the world wide web was now awash with stylists offering image makeover services, and many of them specifically tailored to the needs of 'the great unloved'. I picked a consultant based on location and fee, and a few days later found myself sitting opposite a somewhat stern, humourless lady, with fixed – bordering on rigid – ideas of what a gentleman of my calibre should wear, and the sort of woman I should be trying to attract.

Once again my wardrobe was purged of everything I owned – much of it stuff I actually liked, and another shopping trip arranged to replace those items with new, more stylish, threads, mostly from stores that seemed to employ their staff solely on their ability to sneer, and look at you in that way that makes you wonder whether being born had been a good idea.

For weeks I walked around in clothes that I never really felt comfortable in, and, when I was reasonably certain that I looked as ridiculous as I felt, I sat myself back in front of my computer, and trawled the net again for Image Consultants.

This time I chose more carefully. Location or fee wouldn't be an issue. I'd pay anything, travel anywhere, to find someone who knew what she was doing. And just a few days later I was sitting in front of a mirror, whilst a significantly more charming and glamorous lady than my previous stylist, wafted scarves of various colours in front of me to demonstrate how they changed the appearance of my skin tone. Again my wardrobe underwent a cull, but this time my consultant of choice focused her expertise on my work attire, which she felt was failing to reflect my status as a freelance banking consultant. I tried arguing that I wasn't really all that bothered about impressing my colleagues and clients, that it was my love life that was the issue here, but she waved away my concerns on the grounds that "women find 'power' enormously sexy".

I relented, and a week later I strode purposefully into my client's office, looking as though I was about to renegotiate my contract and ask for a pay rise. Ironically, that's exactly what happened. But whilst my charcoal grey suit and expensive fitted shirts gave my career in banking a kick in the pants, my love life remained in recession.

Maybe it was my new-found negotiation skills, or the unexpected extra cash in my bank balance, but I contacted my stylist again and *insisted* that she do something about my casual wardrobe. One West End shopping trip later and I was kitted out with leather trousers, thin itchy Italian sweaters, itchier designer scarves, a flat cap that was too small for my head and a dry-clean-only raincoat. She was delighted. I was less than convinced. And when I discovered that none of my expensive garments kept out the cold, had any pockets (real ones anyway), or made any noticeable difference to my ability to attract a mate, I thought again of Janine and wondered why she'd been so different.

The conclusion I came to was that Janine's professional 'image consulting' qualifications, had been irrelevant. The only thing that had actually mattered was that she was 'my kind of woman', and she had dressed me as 'her kind of man'. And the more I thought about it the more I became convinced that the other ladies had done the same; turning me into a magnet for brittle, opinionated, aggressive women, or glamorous women seeking slick, Italian-styled, businessmen.

Of course this was all just theory. I couldn't be sure unless I put it to the test. So I placed an ad, with the following title:

**IMAGE CONSULTANT
& PERSONAL SHOPPER REQUIRED**

In it I briefly described my circumstances (that I'd been widowed three years earlier but was ready to start dating again), stressed that I was looking for someone female, young-thinking, with a passion for clothes, style, and what a woman looks for in a man. I asked for a full-length photo, and pointed out that qualifications and even experience were largely unimportant to me, and that I'd ultimately put myself, and my wallet, into the hands of whoever I got on with, and could trust.

I was bowled over with responses. Who'd have thought that so many women would be interested in being paid for their opinions?

I picked my three potentials based on the photos they'd sent me and the chattiness of their emails and arranged 'interviews'. I say interviews – actually I just met each lady for coffee and an informal chat, and eventually I decided on Ellen. She was (and still is), young, cute, funny, scatty, sassy, arty, bursting with positive energy, and a die hard follower of fashion. Moreover she'd recently restyled her boyfriend and all the other members of his band. If ever there was a woman who could help me in the fashion leagues, Ellen had to be it.

And indeed she was.

One shopping trip later, and Ellen somehow managed to put me in clothes that weren't just comfortable, and warm, and had pockets, but were also *me*. She seemed to find the very essence of what I was about and how to present that to the world. Maybe that's what good packaging is all about? Or maybe she just put me in clothes she herself liked. Either way I looked in the mirror and liked what I saw. And within days (yes, days!) I was dating again.

And that was three years ago. And though I insisted on paying Ellen for that initial shopping trip, she only accepted the payment if I agreed that I'd pre-paid for as many future shopping excursions as I felt necessary. And indeed we've been shopping many, many times since.

Let's summarise all this into something you can use.

STOP! ACTION POINT!

Re-styling for the fashionably challenged

1) Time to be honest with yourself again. Could your wardrobe do with a revamp? Is clothes shopping a chore? On a scale of one to ten does your interest in fashion (by which I mean the clothes *you* wear) struggle to get above minus ten?
2) If the answer to any of those questions is 'yes', go in search of your very own stylist. Find someone who
    a. is someone you trust
    b. clearly knows a thing or two about fashion.
3) Consider also the possibility of finding someone who is…
    a. the sex of your desired partner
    b. someone you quite like the look of.
4) Set a budget, then make an appointment to go shopping.
5) Be prepared to do the whole thing again if at first it doesn't work out.

Releasing Your Inner Thespian

For many years I've had a keen interest in photography, and theatre. When I wasn't helping banks bring about the financial downfall of the western world, I was an actor for a small theatre company here in the southeast of England, and a freelance portrait photographer for models, actors and actresses. In my head the two activities are closely related. Taking pictures is nothing more than static theatre. My job is to tell a story with my subject using anything that I have to hand. This makes me the 'director', 'prop master', and occasionally 'wardrobe mistress'. Quite often I take a look at the nondescript clothes that the client has brought with them and decide we can do something better. I dig through the items in the 'dressing up box' and construct an outfit that's a little more interesting.

At times like that, my crippling lack of fashion-confidence I talked about a few pages back never gets a look in. Instead I'm brimming with confidence, and waft away any objections from my client with a wave of my hand.

"Wait until you see the pictures," I say. Usually I'm right.

So why is that? Why is dressing myself so hard when I can apparently do it for other people? Is it because I lack that crucial objectivity when it comes to selecting my own wardrobe? I used to think so – but then one day, as I picked out an outfit for a professional hypnotist who needed some new publicity shots – it occurred to me that maybe it was the 'clothes', or more specifically, the way I looked at them.

When I'm in a departmental store, assessing myself in the changing room mirror, clothes are, well, *fashion*. And I don't really know how to relate to fashion. Fashion makes me think of expensive glossy magazines. The type I can't afford, and wouldn't buy even if I could. To me, those magazine fashion models look ever so slightly dead, and yet somehow they still make me feel gawky and inadequate.

On the other hand, when I'm doing a shoot, or standing in front of an audience, clothes aren't clothes at all – they're a *costume*.

Now a costume – that's something I understand. For an actor a costume is a mask to hide behind. It's also a prop to help them get into character. From a director's perspective – the storyteller – it's an extension of a character's personality. It's a method of communication, where each item of a given outfit are words, assembled together into a phrase or sentence.

If I think of my everyday clothes in terms of a 'costume' then I'm no longer worrying about whether I 'look all right', whether my shoes match my shirt, or whether I've made some other hideous fashion faux pas. Instead, I'm concerned only with the character I'm trying to portray, and the story I want to tell. Right now – right this second – that character is one of full-time author, living a few miles outside London. Slightly geeky. Young at heart. Laid back. Enjoying life. But ever the professional and serious about what he's doing. Now what sort of costume does a character like that wear? How about a pair of well-worn dark blue jeans, with a matching cardigan, over a casual, black & white shirt, under which is just a peek of a t-shirt with some quirky design on the front? A pair of thin-rimmed glasses sets the whole thing off.

If I'm giving a talk then I'll ditch the cardigan in favour of a casual dark grey jacket, put my glasses into the breast pocket, and wear a smiley badge on the lapel.

One day I'll move to warmer climes, and maybe then I'll give my costume a slightly more contemporary, 'New York' feel, with black t-shirts, cargo pants, and thicker-rimmed specs.

This new approach to clothes works well for me. For years I protected myself against the UK winter with whatever came to hand. Most of the time I looked like a cross between a bag lady and a road sweeper, without the charm or elegance of either. Now that I'm adopting the character of 'author' I wear a dark grey, almost military in style, overcoat, black leather gloves, and a large rimmed, black felt fedora hat.

But let's talk about you. What character would you like to portray? The thirty-something, Bridget-Jones-esque, girl-next-door? The hard-working, hard-partying city dweller? The sassy, somehow-single, yummy mummy? The chic geek? If I'm doing my job properly then an image of each of those characters should have popped into your head as I mentioned them. That's an image you can take with you when you go shopping.

Remember; this character *isn't* you. It's the someone you'd like to be. If, for instance, you'd like a little more confidence, then adopt the character of a confident person. Think carefully about what your character of choice looks like, then go shopping for those items. Because as most actors know, a curious thing happens when you spend a significant amount of time 'in character'. After a while the personality of your character seeps through the costume into your soul. It becomes part of you. Takes over. After a while you're not acting any more. You *are* that person. And that's a powerful thing. Because it effectively means you can reinvent yourself from the outside in – just by changing your wardrobe.

Which takes us rather nicely into the next chapter, but before we do, let's book you an appointment with the costume department.

> **STOP! ACTION POINT!**
>
> Getting into character
>
> 1) Think about what character you'd like to portray. This character isn't *you*, it's the person you'd like to be.
> 2) Next think about what that character wears when they're out-and-about, when they're entertaining, and when they're home-alone… write this stuff down. Remember – it's not *you*, it's a character.
> 3) Go buy those clothes!
> 4) Finally, stay in costume at all times. If you have slob-around-the-house clothes throw them away. Or get *new* lounge-around clothes, something that fits in with your new character. Not only will you be 'ready' should you have unexpected guests, but every time you pass a mirror you'll see your character, until eventually it's no longer a character, but a *new you*.

Changing Your Environment

Having changed your image, and rearranged the contents of your head, there's one final slew of changes we can make to improve your attractiveness and overall odds of dating success. I like to categorise these as 'environmental' changes. Now obviously I'm not referring to 'global warming' or your stance on 'renewable energy', I'm talking about where you live, work and socialise, and who you do that with.

Other people

Right back at the start of this book, back when we were discussing the new mindset formula, I touched upon those folks who have a permanent 'poor me' attitude, how their negativity is toxic, and how you should stay as far away from them as possible. They're not the only ones. There are a number of people who you should 'avoid', or avoid talking to – at least when it comes to discussing your love life or lack thereof. Let's take a quick look at who they are.

Friends & Family
Far from being supportive, friends and family can often seem bewilderingly unhelpful in your search for love. From those friends who steadfastly refuse to introduce you to other singletons they know, to the others who will disapprove of anyone you show an interest in, it can sometimes feel like your pals, even your parents, are doing everything they can to ensure you remain single for the rest of your days.

News flash: They probably are.

As a species we're pretty much hardwired to avoid change. If things are working right now, anything that might upset that status quo is perceived as 'bad'– if only on a subconscious level. There's a very good chance that your friends and family like you *exactly* as you are – i.e. *single* – and they want you to stay that way.

Now not all friends (or family) are like this, and those that are might not have made a conscious choice to sabotage your dating efforts, but it's worth bearing in mind if you encounter a response that you weren't expecting.

People in relationships

If you've ever read Helen Fielding's novel 'Bridget Jones's Diary' you'll be familiar with the term 'smug marrieds'; those folks who got hitched and somehow feel qualified to advise you on all aspects of your love-life – or lack of. They'll impart such words of wisdom as 'it'll happen when it happens' or 'as soon as you stop looking you'll find someone', and they'll qualify this advice with the words 'that's what happened to me.'

More common (in my experience) to the 'smug-marrieds' are the 'anti-smug marrieds' – those wedded folks whose advice is along the lines of: "why can't you enjoy being single?" Or: "I'd give my right arm to be in your situation."

Both sets of betrothed individuals are best avoided. The advice they're dishing out isn't really intended for you. They're hoping that somehow their sage words will drift backwards in time and reach a younger version of themselves.

You already know what you want, and being single – or at the very least how you are right now – isn't it. You're also wise enough to know that sitting around actively 'not' doing anything about it, on the off chance that this brings about the result you're hoping for, isn't going to work.

Other Daters

Like the married folk, there are two types of 'dater' in this world:

1) those for whom dating is a heady adventure of excitement and fun, that will inevitably end is marital bliss
2) everyone else.

The first group (and I use the word 'group' in the absolute broadest sense, because if you gathered together all the people in the world for whom dating was a breeze I suspect you could fit them into a Mini Cooper and still have room for their luggage) are basically a version of the smug-marrieds. Nothing they can tell you will be applicable to your experiences. Follow their advice and you're likely to end up frustrated, bitter and twisted. Just seethe quietly to yourself and let them get on with it.

The second group (to which, it has to be said, we are actually a part) are rather more dangerous – for amongst these folks are those who have *become* frustrated, bitter, and twisted.

Like the 'poor me' people we talked about, these people are toxic. *Everything* they tell you will sound familiar. If they choose to impart advice it will inevitably be in the form of warnings; never do this, never tell them that, steer clear of this sort of person, avoid that website. Some will most likely tell you to give up completely – that this dating lark will only end in heartbreak. In short, they'll take any shred of hope you have, and crush it into powder.

It's important to realise that like your friends and family, these sorts of people don't want you to succeed either – they too, want you to stay just the way you are. Why? Because right now you're proof that they're right, that dating really is a mug's game, and that the decision they made to 'give up' was the right one.

They're wrong.

The bottom line is this; Think very carefully before discussing your dating exploits. The reality is there are very few people who can offer you helpful or impartial advice.

Let's wrap this up into a handy Action Point.

> **STOP! ACTION POINT!**
>
> Other People
>
> Beware 'helpful' advice from others. In particular watch out for…
> - Friends and family – often they like you exactly as you are.
> - 'Marrieds' – both the smug and deeply unhappy kind. The advice they have isn't actually for you.
> - Other daters – both the ridiculously successful ones (a different version of the 'smug marrieds') and those who are bitter and twisted (they don't want you to succeed where they've failed).
>
> But do trust…
> - Yourself. You've already decided you want to change. That was a good decision. You'll make many more if you follow your gut instincts.
> - Positive, constructive, practical advice in line with what you've decided you want.

The Right Sofa

A few years back I experienced a minor miracle.

I'd been working for one of the larger financial institutions, and getting on particularly well with a young woman in one of their customer service departments. We had, I suspected, what I've heard ladies refer to as 'chemistry'. And one day, during the course of a rather normal office conversation about what plans each of us had for the weekend, she casually suggested she might be 'passing by' my house, and could 'pop in' for a cuppa.

Now as a man, if I were to say "I could pop in for a cuppa," I'd mean that there's a distinct possibility that I could turn up on your doorstep, with very little warning, and expect you to make us both a cup of tea, or coffee, which we'll drink whilst having a pleasant chat about trivial subjects. But Lord only knows what a woman might mean! Which is why I found myself, that particular Saturday morning, cleaning the flat from top to bottom, in order to prepare for all manner of potential outcomes.

I'll be honest and say that there was one particular outcome I was particularly interested in. One that had necessitated a change of bedding, and a quick check of bedside drawer paraphernalia. But as we balanced tea cups precariously on the arms of our respective chairs, I slowly realised that we were never going to make it upstairs, let alone into the bedroom. Not until we'd reached a certain level of intimacy which was never likely to happen with eight foot of living room between us.

I'd already tried the 'let me give you the guided tour' gambit. The tour had lasted all of ten minutes and finished up back in the lounge. There'd been no reason to stay in the bedroom. And now here we were. That eight foot might as well have been a chasm of continental proportions.

I might as well tell you now that there is no happy ending to this story – least not the one that you, or I come to that, are, were, hoping for. My colleague finished her tea, made her excuses and left. She never 'popped in' again. The subject was never even touched upon. And when my contract ended, I moved on and we lost touch.

You could attribute our lack of romance to a number of things – perhaps she really did just want to "pop in for a cuppa", perhaps there was never any chemistry between us, or perhaps it was simply 'never meant to be' – personally, I blame the furniture.

After she'd gone I surveyed my living room and came to the swift conclusion that my 'bachelor pad' was doing a damn fine job of making sure I stayed that way – a bachelor.

The problem was this; with only one arm chair and a rather small two-seater sofa to choose from, myself and any guests would invariably end up seated in separate chairs, opposite each other. Sharing the tiny sofa would be great for a cosy night in front of the TV, but completely impractical, bordering on awkward and inappropriate, if you wanted to 'chat'. Unless there was a major overhaul in terms of seating options, tea and coffee was as far as any future romance was likely to get.

The very next day I was visiting furniture stores, and not long after this revelation my lounge underwent something of a transformation.

Now, were you to 'pop in for tea' you'd find a stylish corner sofa; roomy enough so that we wouldn't be squashed together, but intimate enough that I could just shuffle a little closer, whilst we browse my stamp collection,

And if I kick off my shoes, sit myself in the corner, put my feet up, spread my arms along the back of the chair – I could do so without invading your personal space. Although if you want to kick off your shoes, and put your feet up… well, you could rest them on top of mine if you like. And suddenly here we are, getting all cosy as the afternoon drifts by. Some gurus call this 'comfort building', I like to call it 'romance'.

And yes. I've done this.

Several times[8].

Some Dating Gurus say it takes a minimum of seven hours of steady 'comfort-building' to "escalate a fledgling relationship to the intimacy threshold". In other words, seven hours – minimum – of gradually getting closer and closer, both metaphorically and physically, to the point where the two of you transcend from acquaintances to 'something more'. You're going to need a place to do that. And sitting on opposite sides of a room sipping tea, simply isn't going to cut it!

Neither is a noisy room. A smelly room. A cold room. A room where the door could fly open at any moment and any combination of house mates, parents, pets, or children, can come charging in.

Make time to take stock of your environment.

Let's do that now.

---

[8] Although I don't actually have a stamp collection – though I'd definitely have invested in one if I thought it might work. You get the idea I'm sure.

> **STOP! ACTION POINT!**
>
> ## The Right Sofa
>
> Long before you ever get to the point where you discover there might be an issue, imagine how events might play out should someone 'pop by' for a cuppa, or 'come in for a coffee' after a particularly successful date. If you can foresee any problems, now's the time to do something about it.

Getting Out There

For much of my life I've been a fan of Kylie Minogue.

I know what you're thinking and you're right; I like her for all the obvious male reasons – she's cute, pretty, she occasionally doesn't wear very much – but there's more to her than that. OK, I confess I'm not basing this on much – the odd interview, her cameo appearance in the Vicar of Dibley – but there's only so much a person can fake. Sooner or later the façade slips, and when it does, if you're paying attention, you get to glimpse the real person underneath. And from what I've seen, the real Kylie is an interesting, funny, caring, feeling, beautiful (on the inside) woman. She's this 'normal girl' who settles down in front of the TV on a Friday night, with a glass of Chardonnay, and croons to soppy love songs when she thinks nobody's listening. Who wouldn't be attracted to someone like that? And if there'd been any justice in the world, then somehow events should have conspired to bring the two of us together.

Some might say my chances of meeting Kylie, let alone getting her into my life, are slim, non-existent even. But that's just negative thinking. I had it all worked out: I'd have been at home one Saturday or Sunday afternoon, dressed in my very smartest togs due to a washing backlog, when, quite by chance, the doorbell would have rung and a distressed Kylie would be standing in the porch.

"I'm terribly sorry," she'd say. "I've just broken down and this piece of junk," (holding the latest mobile phone for me to see) "has chosen this precise moment to run out of juice. Could I use your phone?"

And, being the perfect gentleman, I'd wave her in with a heady mixture of sympathy about shoddy phone batteries, and absolutely no hint that I recognise her at all.

Then, while she sits on my sofa recovering from the shock of being told by whatever car recovery company rock stars use these days that they "couldn't possibly get anyone to her in under three hours", I'd breeze in from the kitchen with a chamomile tea, and she'd tell me how the whole celeb thing has just become too much, how soothing the tea is, and please, call her 'Minnie' and ... oh, could I just hold her for a while because she really needs a hug right now.

I mentioned this to my wife, Kate. She laughed. And laughed, and laughed. And when she'd finished laughing, she brushed away a tear and suggested I ought to write it down.

"That," she said, "would make a very entertaining first chapter of a novel."[9]

I smiled and shrugged. "Maybe," I agreed. I've learnt to accept compliments whenever they're offered. But it wasn't a compliment. What Kate had found so ludicrous, was how I hoped my life would play out. Maybe not with Kylie, and maybe not some convoluted car / phone break-down scenario – but something equally unlikely. Truth is, for the longest time I was relying on it.

I've been putting off writing this section because 'getting out there' is something that I struggle with.

I wouldn't go as far to say I'm agoraphobic[10] but those who know me well also know that I'm not particularly keen on 'leaving the house', for any reason, but particularly not to 'meet new people'. It's the 'meeting' aspect I find uncomfortable, not the people.

So the idea of going to a venue specifically to talk to people I don't know in order to increase the odds of

---

[9] As it turned out, Kate was right. Check out my debut novel "The Good Guy's Guide To Getting The Girl".
[10] Typically thought of as a 'fear of the outside', the actual definition is an anxiety about being in places or situations from which escape might be difficult (or embarrassing), or in which help may not be available in the event of a Panic Attack or panic-like symptoms.

creating friendships that might lead to more... well that's kinda terrifying. None the less, like the laws of physics there's no escape from this law of romance:

> **IN ORDER TO MEET SOMEONE SPECIAL**
> **YOU HAVE TO *MEET* SOMEONE SPECIAL**

Sitting at home, alone, isn't going to work. You will never ever find love, lust, or romance, unless you're prepared to leave the house. At least once. And in reality, many, many times.

If, like the younger version of me, you're hoping for a miracle to happen let the grown up me pop that bubble for you right now. Miracles are in short supply. Worse still they're distributed in an almost random fashion. There is no 'eligibility' for miracles – least not the way you think there should be. Life just doesn't work that way.

Now I'm not suggesting you *have* to start frequenting night clubs, join a ceroc dance class, or look up speed dating events in your area – but if any one of those things doesn't appal you too much that would definitely be a good start.

What I am going to suggest is that you find some way of leaving the house, once a week, to be amongst people you feel comfortable with, and where there's a reasonably good chance of people you don't know showing up.

So you might consider an evening class, or a social club. Take up a hobby (painting, writing, music, amateur dramatics, after dinner speaking, furniture restoring), hell – start frequenting your local coffee shop if necessary, just don't sit yourself in a corner and bury your face in a book.

Once out the door you need to *force yourself* to talk to people, *especially* people you don't know, *even if* you don't find them attractive. You don't have to introduce yourself formally and interrogate everyone you meet, but a simple 'hello' followed by some sort of comment or question ("I'm not in your way, am I?" "Did you make these cakes?" "I'm fairly new – do you come here often?") will:

1) build your confidence
2) increase the odds of a miracle happening.

And that's the funny thing about miracles. The less you rely on them, the more likely they seem to happen.

> **STOP! ACTION POINT!**
>
> Getting Out There
>
> **IN ORDER TO MEET SOMEONE SPECIAL
> YOU HAVE TO *MEET* SOMEONE SPECIAL**
>
> If you want romance in your life you are going to need to leave the house, and talk to a stranger. Probably more than once.
>
> Consider the following:
>
> - The more you leave the house and talk to people the more likely you are to 'bump into' that special someone.
> - Aim to leave the house at least once a week (not just for work or shopping)
> - Consider joining a club or social group
> - Talk to strangers whenever you get a chance, regardless of whether you find them attractive. Do it for the practice.

Start Dating And Stop Waiting

Well congratulations. You've almost reached the end of the book, and may I be the first to say how attractive you're looking!

How are you doing with that last Action Point? Are you leaving the house on a regular basis? Are you talking to strangers? Are you ready to take that last step one stage further? Are you ready… to start dating?

Before I started on my quest for happiness, I was using my problem solving skills to figure out what actually works when it comes to courting the opposite sex. From the pen-pal clubs of the early eighties, to the lonely heart newspaper ads of the nineties, from postal dating services to the more formal introduction agencies – there hasn't been a dating service that I haven't tried!

And after many, many years of seemingly making every dating mistake there is – scouring every scrap of scientific research I could get my hands on – I finally cracked it. There's love in my life. And it wasn't an accident.

So let me see if I can impart some of that knowledge to you now. Here are my top five tips for dating success.

Dating Tip Number 1: What do you want?
Figuring out who it is you're looking for is probably *the* most effective thing you can do to kick start your love life. You might think (as I used to) that you can't afford to be picky, that finding someone who doesn't repel you too much and is content to remain in your company might be the best you can hope for. I'm here to tell you that the reverse is true.

After months, possibly even years, of less-than-satisfactory relationships with long periods of nothing in-between, I sat down and wrote out what I actually wanted. A list of qualities that I hoped for in my ideal person. And about six weeks later I met my wife, Kate.

Now – that's not the whole story, obviously. There were a few stages between writing my 'perfect woman shopping list' and choosing to sit next to this beautiful blonde I spied from across the room, but a few months into our relationship I looked back at that list and I was amazed at just how many of the criteria Kate met. Coincidence? Perhaps. But for the time it would take you to create your own list isn't it worth the effort?

Dating Tip Number 2: Go online!
By my calculations online dating websites are responsible for one in five marriages[11]. Include relationships that haven't got as far as the altar, throw in the likes of facebook and other social media websites, and I estimate 50 percent of all romances probably start on the internet. Which means that simply using your computer to meet people could double your chances of dating success[12].

Dating Tip Number 3: Pick a good dating website
There are a LOT of dating websites out there – finding a *good* one can be a challenge. My current[13] feelings are the free-ones can be just as good, sometimes better, than the paid-ones. For extra oomph pick a site that does some form of compatibility matching!

Dating Tip Number 4: To meet 'the one', you must first meet 'the many'
Very, very few people go on one date and hit the jackpot first time. In fact, in the years I've been chatting to people about this stuff I've never met anyone who has.

---

[11] Check my numbers at howtostartdatingandstopwaiting.com.
[12] That's assuming that you took the advice in the last section and you're already leaving the house once a week and meeting people in real life.
[13] January 2014

Dating is a numbers game. If you find someone you like online send them a message. If they respond toss a couple more messages back and forth. If you still like them arrange to meet. *Meanwhile*; continue to browse the dating sites, continue to send messages, continue arranging dates. Exclusivity should be reserved for that special someone you've dated more than once, in real life, and even then only if you want to.

As well as a numbers game, dating is a skill. The more dates you go on the better you'll get.

Dating Tip Number 5: Have fun!
Dating is tough. It has to be said. Some days it can feel like a slog. But if it *always* feels like a slog, if it's tough without being the slightest bit pleasurable, well, then you're doing something wrong!

Try changing your mindset. Dating *can* be fun. An adventure. Exciting. It's a little like a lottery; Sometimes it's just OK. Sometimes it's better than OK. Occasionally it's a total disaster, but every now and then it's magical. And those moments make up for everything.

Secondly, make sure you're doing things you actually enjoy. For me, a good first date takes place in a coffee shop, if it's going really well I might suggest wandering across to the pub over the road. Dinners and first dates don't mix well. But that's just me. Maybe you're into bungy jumping, or white water rafting or long walks in the countryside. Picking an activity you enjoy will significantly increase the chances of your first date going well.

If all this talk of dating has got you fired up and keen to get out there, well, good for you! Fly my pretty! I wish you all the success in the world.

If on the other hand you want to delve into the detail behind the five tips above, pick my brain for more nuggets of dating gems, or need a little more hand holding, then I have some very good news. This book is a companion guide – a prequel if you like – to a much larger tome. *How To Start Dating And Stop Waiting* is your one-stop guide to successful dating, helping you find love, lust or romance, now.

Are you ready for more?

'How To Start Dating And Stop Waiting'
is available in paperback, audio, and as an ebook,
from amazon & wherever you got this book from.
Find out more at
www.howtostartdatingandstopwaiting.com

You Still Here?

And there was me thinking that last page would generate a frenzy of dating related activities! Ah, but I can see from the smile on your face that today is a day for doing something fun. Tell me, are you feeling happier yet? Are you beating those demons?

And whilst we're on the subject, how's that new image coming along? Are people noticing you again? Have you lost a little weight? Is that a new pair of glasses? And have you changed the furniture? Either way you're looking good. Good for you.

It's only been a short book, but it feels to me like we've covered a lot of ground. I hope you feel the same way.

Let's wrap this up.

Final Remarks

"Beauty is a form of genius – is higher, indeed, than genius, as it needs no explanation. It is of the great facts of the world, like sunlight, or spring-time, or the reflection in dark waters of that silver shell we call the moon. It cannot be questioned. It has its divine right of sovereignty. It makes princes of those who have it."
Lord Henry, from Oscar Wilde's novel, "The Portrait of Dorian Gray"

For the longest time I used to think that attractiveness and beauty – at least when talking about people – were somehow related, that if you had beauty, you'd automatically be attractive, or that to be attractive required a certain level of beauty. These days, I'm not so sure.

In years gone by I've met more than a few 'beautiful' people; ladies with lovely figures, men with chiselled features, stunning individuals who at first almost take your breath simply by 'being'. And then, in a moment, sometimes just the time it took for them to utter a few words, that attraction evaporated, and any desire I may have had to be near them – was gone.

Fortunately for me, I've known many more people, some whom might have seemed really quite ordinary at first, but change that sweater, change the subject, see them smile, hear them laugh, and suddenly – I'm feeling drawn to this person! I'm finding reasons to stay in their company. They've become 'attractive'.

All of which leads me to suspect that not only is attraction more powerful than beauty, but that the two aren't connected at all.

Attraction is available to anyone.

Everyone.

Go. Be attractive.

Best wishes,
Peter

If You've Enjoyed This Book…

If you've enjoyed what you read and you'd like to 'spread the word', then here are a few ways you can do just that.

Review the book
Positive reviews are always welcome. Pop back to wherever you bought this book from to leave a glowing five star endorsement, or visit Amazon (.co.uk | .com).

Like the Facebook Page
If you're on Facebook pop along to the Facebook page (facebook.com/frominvisibletoirresistible), and click the LIKE button (up there at the top).

Your 'friends' will be able to see that you're a fan, and you might see the occasional comments from other readers in your feed, as well as a daily post from us. Nothing too intrusive, I promise.

Feel free to post a comment or two yourself.

Follow me on Twitter
If you're more of a twitterer I tweet under the handle @peterjonesauth. The odd re-tweet would be most appreciated. Follow me at: twitter.com/peterjonesauth.

Got a blog or a podcast?
A mention of the book, or a link to frominvisibletoirresistible.com would be most appreciated.

If you'd me to write a guest post for your blog, or interview me for your podcast, just drop me a line.

Tell a friend
And finally, one of the hardest things for any author to achieve is 'word of mouth' recommendations. Next time you find yourself sitting next to someone who's telling you how hard dating is, do them, yourself, and us a favour – tell them about this book!

If you can do any of these things, I'd like to offer you our heartfelt thanks.

And whilst I'm in the 'thanking' mood...

Acknowledgements

In no particular order I'd really like to thank:

Jules – for her endless wisdom, friendship, and making the really important stuff in my life 'happen' whilst I continue to gamble it all. I couldn't have done this without you.

Della – for all her love, support, advice, help and reminding me, frequently, that I am in fact 'living the dream'. Who knew!

My dear friend Wendy – for her endless passion and encouragement.

My agent Becky – for believing in me, this book, and for fighting my corner more than once.

And to you, dear reader, for taking a chance on this quirky little book.

Thank you all.

About the Author

Peter Jones started professional life as a particularly rubbish graphic designer, followed by a stint as a mediocre petrol pump attendant. After that he got embroiled in the murky world of credit card banking. Fun times.

Now, Peter spends his days – most of them, anyway – writing.

He is the author of three and a half popular self-help books on the subjects of happiness, staying slim and dating. If you're overweight, lonely, or unhappy – he's definitely your guy.

His latest book "*The Good Guy's Guide to Getting The Girl*" is his début novel. It wasn't a 'historical' romance when he started out – it just took that long to write. The sequel is currently sitting on his desk. Waiting to be edited. Occasionally it seems to wink.

Peter doesn't own a large departmental store and probably isn't the same guy you've seen on the TV show Dragons' Den.

Find out more about Peter Jones,
his books, speaking engagements and workshops
at www.peterjonesauthor.com

Also In The Series

Also In The Series

Change your life today…

It started with *How To Do Everything And Be Happy*, now it's a best-selling series. If you're unhappy, lonely or overweight, Peter Jones might just be the man for you

The books:

How To Do Everything And Be Happy
Your step-by-step, straight-talking guide to creating happiness in your life!

How To Eat Loads And Stay Slim
Your diet-free guide to losing weight without feeling hungry!

How To Start Dating And Stop Waiting
Your heartbreak-free guide to finding love, lust, or romance – now!

From Invisible To Irresistible
Your twelve step action plan to attracting the man or woman of your dreams!

*Available in paperback,
for your e-reading device, or in audio.
Find out more at
www.HowToDoEverythingAndBeHappy.com*

Also Available

The Good Guy's Guide To Getting The Girl

The debut novel from Peter Jones

The Good Guy's Guide To Getting The Girl

"Liz. Where do I start?
I suppose the end is as good a place as any."

Boxing Day, 1997: Jason Smith, 29, and self-confessed 'good guy', is single again. And now that he is, it seems all the single girls – the 'Melanie Jacksons' of this world – are in short supply. Or are they? Has Jason stumbled on a foolproof way to find the girl of his dreams?

Both aided and hindered by his beer-drinking best buddy and reluctant father-to-be Alex, and his ever-wise, ever-sarcastic colleague Sian, 'The Good Guy's Guide to Getting The Girl' follows Jason on a voyage of self-discovery as he experiences the highs and lows of trying to meet one's soul mate at the turn of the millennium.

Visit amazon to
buy the book
and find out more Peter Jones at
PeterJonesAuthor.com

For a complete list of other great titles from
soundhaven books,
both fiction and non-fiction,
visit
www.soundhaven.com